CW00958767

LESSONS ON LIVING FROM
DANIEL

A devotional by
WOODROW KROLL

BACK TO THE BIBLE
Publishing

DANIEL
published by Back to the Bible Publishing
©1998 by Woodrow Kroll

International Standard Book Number
0-8474-0692-X

Edited by Rachel Derowitsch
Cover design by Robert Greuter
& Associates

For information:
BACK TO THE BIBLE
POST OFFICE BOX 82808
LINCOLN, NEBRASKA 68501

1 2 3 4 5 6 7 8—04 03 02 01 00 99 98

Printed in the USA

CONTENTS

DAY 1

Daniel 1:1–2

In the third year of the reign of Jehoiakim king of Judah, Nebuchadnezzar king of Babylon came to Jerusalem and besieged it. And the Lord gave Jehoiakim king of Judah into his hand, with some of the articles of the house of God, which he carried into the land of Shinar to the house of his god; and he brought the articles into the treasure house of his god.

Roosting Chickens

My father often said, "Just wait. The chickens will come home to roost." By that he meant sooner or later, every transgressor will experience the consequences of his behavior. Just as surely as a chicken finds its way back to the henhouse at night, the penalty of sin finally will come home to every sinner.

Daniel lived in a time when the chickens were coming home to roost. The northern kingdom, Israel, already had reaped the results of its transgressions and had been taken into captivity by the Assyrians in 722 B.C. God spared the southern kingdom, Judah, for more than 100 years after Israel's fall. But the leaders and people of Judah continued in their wicked ways, with King Manasseh (697-642 B.C.) being the most corrupt of all (2 Kings 23:26). Baal worship, divination and even human sacrifices were a part of

4

daily life. God finally used the Babylonians to chastise His people by taking them into exile, first in 605 B.C. (when Daniel, among others, was taken), then again in 597 B.C. and finally in 586 B.C., when Jerusalem was destroyed.

God is gracious and merciful, but He is also holy and just. This requires Him to confront sin, which destroys the people He loves. Unless He can turn the hearts of His people from their wicked ways, they will not only harm themselves but also miss out on an intimate relationship with Him. This is more than God can tolerate.

If you are being chastised for sin, remember that it is because God loves you and wants to turn your heart back toward Him. Be grateful that God cares enough about you to want the very best for you, even if it means temporary pain. Remember, temporary pain can bring permanent blessing.

God's discipline is ultimately an act of love.

Reflections/Prayer Requests

_____

_____

_____

_____

_____

DAY 2

Daniel 1:3–4

*Then the king instructed Ashpenaz,
the master of his eunuchs, to bring some
of the children of Israel and some of the
king's descendants and some of the nobles,
young men in whom there was no blemish,
but good-looking, gifted in all wisdom,
possessing knowledge and quick to understand, who had ability to serve in the king's
palace, and whom they might teach the lan-
guage and literature of the Chaldeans.*

Only the Best

Thomas à Kempis, the German mystic and author of *The Imitation of Christ*, observed, "The devil does not tempt unbelievers and sinners who are already his own." Satan only wants what belongs to God—and he wants God's very best.

When King Nebuchadnezzar came to deport the first group of God's people, he was not willing to settle for just anyone. He instructed Ashpenaz, the master of his eunuchs, to bring only those young men who were of noble birth, good-looking and intelligent. He didn't want the local shepherd boys; he wanted the cream of the crop. His desire was to take God's very best and turn them into his own servants.

The more determined a Christian is to be the very best God can make him or her, the more such a person should expect and prepare for Satan's subtle attacks. The moment we decide to get serious about having a daily quiet time, we can be sure that Satan will place as many obstacles in our path as possible. When we choose to follow God's call into lifetime Christian service, Satan will make certain that all the reasons why this should not be done will surface.

Are you determined to serve God? Then don't be surprised by Satan's attacks. Instead, take up the shield of faith, which is able to quench the Devil's "fiery darts" (Eph. 6:16). Rejoice that Satan considers you one of God's best, but trust God to take care of you when you become one of his targets.

Satan doesn't target the mediocre; he wants the best.

Reflections/Prayer Requests

_____

_____

_____

_____

_____

_____

_____

_____

_____

DAY 3

Daniel 1:6–7

Now from among those of the sons of Judah were Daniel, Hananiah, Mishael, and Azariah. To them the chief of the eunuchs gave names: he gave Daniel the name Belteshazzar; to Hananiah, Shadrach; to Mishael, Meshach; and to Azariah, Abed-Nego.

Changed Names

Some people assume new names to disguise their identity. For example, Samuel Langhorne Clemens took the pen name of Mark Twain. Mary Ann Evans took the masculine pen name of George Eliot. Other people change their names when they move to a new country to make them more pronounceable. For example, de Revoire became Revere, and Yitzchak became Hitchcock. Yet others feel a different name will make them more memorable. Thus, Erich Weiss became Harry Houdini, and Betty Joan Perske is better known as Lauren Bacall.

Ashpenaz, the chief of the eunuchs, also desired to change the names of the young men taken from Jerusalem. After all, it just wouldn't do to have people serving in Nebuchadnezzar's court with names like Daniel ("God is my judge"), Hananiah ("Jehovah was favored"), Mishael ("who is like God") and Azariah ("strengthened by Jehovah"). These names honored the God of Israel, so Ashpenaz changed them to reflect Babylonian gods. Daniel became Belteshazzar ("Bel protect his life"), Hananiah was called Shadrach ("command of Akur"), Azariah became Abed-Nego ("servant of Nebo"), and Mishael was renamed Meshach (a possible corruption of the name Maraduk, another Babylonian deity).

Society today is also good at changing the name of things that honor God. Having standards is now called intolerance. Taking a stand for what you believe is understood as fanaticism. The change works the other way as well. Adultery is called an affair. Drunkenness is now alcoholism. But don't be taken in by a change in names. God's principles haven't changed.

Guide your life by God's Word, and you will be pleasing to the Lord no matter what the world calls it. After all, what's in a name? Not much if God isn't in it.

Changing the name doesn't change the truth.

Reflections/Prayer Requests

_____

_____

_____

_____

_____

DAY 4

Daniel 1:8

But Daniel purposed in his heart that he would not defile himself with the portion of the king's delicacies, nor with the wine which he drank; therefore he requested of the chief of the eunuchs that he might not defile himself.

Committed to Purity

Some hunters are totally sold out to hunting. They suffer all kinds of discomfort in order to enjoy their hobby. Many sports fans are totally absorbed by games, whether baseball, football or soccer or anything else. Whatever else might be taking place, they're in the stands or in front of the TV rooting for their favorite team. Likewise, some businessmen can think of nothing but their business. Everything takes second place to being successful in their chosen profession.

But Daniel was sold out in a different way. He was totally committed to maintaining his purity. The drink and rich foods of Babylon in all probability were very tasty, but, prepared by pagan cooks, they surely would not have met the strict Jewish dietary laws. To have eaten these delicacies would have caused Daniel and his friends ritual impurity. And in Daniel's heart, the culinary pleasures he might have enjoyed were not worth the price of moral pollution.

Today we live in a time of gross immorality. We live in a sea of sensual indulgence. Sex appeal is used to promote everything from cars to shoes. Images that would have made our grandparents blush are brazenly displayed on billboards. Standards that once protected society from its own carnal appetites have been long abandoned. Therefore, it's more important than ever that those who follow Christ commit themselves to maintaining their purity, as Daniel did.

Resolve in your own heart, even before you face temptation, that you will make purity your highest priority. Expect to be tempted, but determine that, with God's help, you will stay undefiled and never waver. The short-lived pleasures of immorality are not worth the price.

When purity is not a priority it is a casualty.

Reflections/Prayer Requests

_____

_____

_____

_____

_____

_____

_____

DAY 5

Daniel 1:14–15

So he consented with them in this matter, and tested them ten days. And at the end of ten days their countenance appeared better and fatter in flesh than all the young men who ate the portion of the king's delicacies.

Honoring God

Eric Liddell, a young Scottish ministerial student, was the best sprinter in the British Empire. He was favored to win the 100-meter race in the 1924 Paris Olympics. A few weeks before the Games, however, he learned that the preliminary 100-meter races were scheduled for a Sunday afternoon. Liddel considered participating in Sunday sports dishonoring to the Lord. His friends then began to notice during the weeks prior to the Olympics that he excused himself after dinner each evening and would return home hours later, exhausted.

A few weeks later the whole world discovered his secret. He had spent those evening hours practicing for another event that was scheduled for a weekday but which required a different type of speed and endurance. On the closing day of the Olympics, he stood on the winner's platform and received the Gold Medal as the 400-meter champion. By putting God's honor first, Liddel himself received honor.

Daniel was faced with a similar choice. To him and his friends, partaking of the king's refreshments would be shameful before the Lord. Bravely they chose to honor God. When they did so, God honored them. After ten days of eating only vegetables, they were in better condition than those who had eaten of the king's food.

The pressure to compromise is tremendous. Many people tell us that unless we choose to follow the world's standards, we'll never get ahead. If we don't drink socially, we'll never rub elbows with the influential people who can make our business a success. If we aren't willing to engage in premarital sex, we'll never meet a potential marriage partner.

Obviously, Satan skews such thinking. If we choose to honor God with our lives, He will honor us by meeting our needs. Put God's honor first, and your honor will never suffer.

Honor God and He will never dishonor you.

Reflections/Prayer Requests

_____

_____

_____

_____

DAY 6

Daniel 2:8–10

*The king answered and said, "I know
for certain that you would gain time,
because you see that my decision is firm:
if you do not make known the dream to me,
there is only one decree for you! For you
have agreed to speak lying and corrupt
words before me till the time has changed.
Therefore tell me the dream, and I shall know
that you can give me its interpretation."
The Chaldeans answered the king, and said,
"There is not a man on earth who can tell the
king's matter; therefore no king, lord, or ruler
has ever asked such things of any magician,
astrologer, or Chaldean."*

No Man on Earth

In the realm of fairy tales, straw is
spun into gold, frogs turn into Prince
Charmings, and pumpkins become royal
coaches with mice for footmen. But these
things are not possible in our world.
Human beings in the real world have limitations.

Such limitations caused problems for
the wise men of Babylon. King Nebuchadnezzar had dreamed a disturbing
dream. Immediately he issued a call for
his magicians, astrologers, sorcerers and
Chaldeans. Not trusting these advisers to
give him a true answer, however, he de-
manded they first tell him the dream and
then interpret it. If they didn't, he said,

they would be cut in pieces and their houses would be made an ash heap (2:5). Of course, their response was, "No ruler has ever asked such a thing!" This was an impossible request.

Often in our world we encounter things that are simply impossible. No man on earth can do them. Fortunately, as believers in Christ, our resources extend beyond earthly man; we have a Heavenly Father. God can do what no man can do. He said of Himself, "Behold, I am the LORD, the God of all flesh. Is there anything too hard for Me?" (Jer. 32:27).

Are you facing an impossible task today? Is there trouble in your life that is greater than any person on earth can resolve? Then look to God. He can do what others cannot. He'll do it for you.

God can do anything but fail.

Reflections/Prayer Requests

_____

_____

_____

_____

_____

_____

_____

_____

DAY 7

Daniel 2:11

*"It is a difficult thing that the king requires,
and there is no other who can tell it
to the king except the gods, whose
dwelling is not with flesh."*

God With Us

A farmer was plowing his field when he noticed a very large anthill out in the middle of the field. It was evident that hundreds, perhaps thousands, of ants had worked long and hard to build this magnificent edifice. Now, in a short time, his plow would destroy it, along with many of the ants that lived there. *I wonder*, he thought, *how I might communicate with them. I could write them a letter, but they couldn't read it. I could stand near their home and urge them to flee from destruction. But they wouldn't understand me.* Then he realized there was really only one solution—he would have to become an ant and dwell among them.

The gods the Babylonians worshiped were deities who kept themselves apart from their worshipers. At best, they communicated only through the priests and priestesses who served them in the temples. It took the true God to devise a meaningful way to communicate with His people. John 1:14 tells us, "And the Word became flesh and dwelt among us, and we beheld His glory, the glory as of the only begotten of the Father, full of grace and truth."

Christians have the privilege of communicating with a God who is not way off in some distant place. Instead, He is as near as our next breath (Acts 17:28). We don't have to go to a special place to speak with Him; He dwells in us and delights to fellowship with us. By becoming one of us and dying for our sins, He has made it possible for us to carry every burden to Him and leave it there.

Rejoice that God wrapped Himself in human flesh and dwelt among us. Give thanks that He is only a prayer away. Whatever question or concern you may have, come to Him. His Word and His Spirit are always available to help you find the answer.

God is so near that the faintest prayer can reach Him.

Reflections/Prayer Requests

_____

_____

_____

_____

_____

_____

DAY 8

Daniel 2:12–14

*For this reason the king was angry
and very furious, and gave a command
to destroy all the wise men of Babylon.
So the decree went out, and they began
killing the wise men; and they sought Daniel
and his companions, to kill them. Then with
counsel and wisdom Daniel answered Arioch,
the captain of the king's guard, who had gone
out to kill the wise men of Babylon.*

Speaking Without Anger

Anger has become a major problem in our society, especially when associated with driving. Between 1990 and 1997, 250,000 people were killed in traffic accidents. The U.S. Department of Transportation estimates that two-thirds of these road fatalities were caused by drivers who were angry. They not only lost their temper, but they lost their lives as well.

When Daniel was confronted with the king's edict, it could have given way to anger. The king's demands were unreasonable. Who ever heard of telling the dream as well as giving the interpretation? Furthermore, it was unfair. Why destroy all the wise men when not everyone had been given the opportunity to redeem himself? But Daniel knew better than to give way to such futile passions. Instead, he answered with "counsel and wisdom."

To his credit, Daniel first sought information. He checked out the facts to find out what lay behind this seemingly unreasonable edict. Then he spoke with wisdom. Daniel took the time to understand the situation and then offered a practical solution that would both meet the king's need and save the lives of many innocent people.

Anger can be terribly devastating, especially for Christians. Not only do they suffer the same consequences unbelievers do when they lose their temper, but they also tarnish their testimony before a watching world.

If you struggle with anger, learn to seek counsel and then speak with wisdom. Get the facts straight. Give yourself time to think about the consequences of your anger. And then, rather than waste your energy on a fit of rage and bring shame to the Lord, ask God to show you how you can resolve the situation for His glory.

Anger isn't always wrong, but it's seldom profitable.

Reflections/Prayer Requests

_____

_____

_____

_____

DAY 9

He Removes Kings

Robert Ingersoll, a 19th-century American politician and atheist, said, "The universe is all the God there is." Ingersoll lectured widely about his belief that God did not exist. Yet Ingersoll is gone and God is still here. Bertrand Russell, a British philosopher and social critic, proclaimed, "My own view on religion is that it is a disease born of fear and is a source of untold misery to the human race." Russell has stepped into eternity and is no doubt rethinking his view.

Daniel realized that even powerful dictators like King Nebuchadnezzar are no match for the omnipotent, omniscient God of the universe. Though they swagger in their own self-importance, the time comes when God removes them and raises up others to take their place. As the seasons of nature come and go, so even the most authoritarian leaders pass from the scene. Though they may seem to hold the power of life or death over millions, they themselves are subject to the desires of Him who holds their lives in His hand.

The pages of history are filled with individuals who have either denied or defied the God of heaven and earth. Yet without exception, they have been confronted with the realization that they were only mortal and posed no real threat to God. While they confidently basked in the power of their independence, God retained the ability to lift them up or cast them down.

Do not fear those who mock God. They have no more power than what God will allow. When you hear someone railing on God, remember that it is only divine grace that keeps that person from destruction. If God were not so good, atheists would have no opportunity to talk.

Man's decisions seem final until God decides otherwise.

Reflections/Prayer Requests

_____

_____

_____

_____

_____

_____

DAY 10

Daniel 2:28

"But there is a God in heaven who reveals se-crets, and He has made known to King Neb-uchadnezzar what will be in the latter days. Your dream, and the visions of your head upon your bed, were these."

Mysteries Revealed

Many people love a good mystery story. With avid interest they follow the twists and turns of plots woven by such master mystery writers as Agatha Christie or Mary Higgins Clark. Yet there comes a point when the mystery needs to be revealed. Who really did it? Was it the butler? Per-haps the jilted lover? Maybe the upstairs maid? Unless the mystery is revealed, the whole point of the story is lost.

God never leaves a mystery unresolved either. As Daniel was faced with the need to unravel the strange and disturbing dream of King Nebuchadnezzar, God sup-plied the answers. What could not be known by any other means, God revealed to Daniel at the appropriate time. Nothing is hidden from God's sight; no answers are beyond His understanding. When the need to know is there, God always provides the information.

Life is filled with mysteries. We ask ourselves, *Why did this young missionary die in a car accident?* On the surface, it appears to be a mystery. *Why did I develop cancer while an ungodly neighbor lives a long and healthy life?* The answer doesn't seem obvious. *Why was my child born with birth defects while my friend's child is healthy?* There are no easy explanations.

If you are struggling with a mystery, if you have more questions than answers, wait patiently. It's hard, but you must believe that God will not keep the answer hidden forever. A day will come, perhaps on earth or maybe in heaven, when you will understand. Some day all the mysteries that plague us, all the plaintive wails of "Why?" will be answered. Until then, trust the Divine Writer. At just the right time, He'll reveal the secret.

God is a God of revelation, not a God of secrets.

Reflections/Prayer Requests

_____

_____

_____

_____

_____

_____

_____

_____

DAY 11

Daniel 2:44

"And in the days of these kings the God of heaven will set up a kingdom which shall never be destroyed; and the kingdom shall not be left to other people; it shall break in pieces and consume all these kingdoms, and it shall stand forever."

The Forever Kingdom

Three huge gates lead into the Cathedral of Milan in Italy. Over one gate is an inscription in marble under a beautiful floral bouquet that says, "The things that please us are temporary." Over another gate is a cross with the inscription, "The things that disturb us are temporary." Over the central gate, however, is a large inscription that says, "The things that are important are eternal."

As Daniel shared with Nebuchadnezzar the interpretation of the king's dream, he revealed that God had shown him that many kingdoms would rise and fall. As mighty and magnificent as Babylon was under the reign of Nebuchadnezzar, it would someday be replaced by an even more magnificent kingdom. Yet even this kingdom would come to an end, and others would rise after it. Finally, however, God would set up His kingdom, which would last forever.

It's so easy to get caught up in things that are here today but gone tomorrow. They look so solid and permanent, yet they are temporary and inconsequential. Thus, we find ourselves chasing changing fads and grasping at straws as they are blown about by the wind. Only when we fix our hearts and minds on the things of God do we find true stability. God's kingdom will never end.

Don't waste your time on things that are only temporary. Neither your pleasures nor your problems will last forever. Count on it. Fix your mind on things that are above and invest in things that are eternal. When you look to God and His kingdom, you look to what really matters.

Don't let a fascination with the temporal diminish your focus on the eternal.

Reflections/Prayer Requests

_____

_____

_____

_____

_____

_____

_____

_____

DAY 12

Daniel 3:17–18

"If that is the case, our God whom we serve is able to deliver us from the burning fiery furnace, and He will deliver us from your hand, O king. But if not, let it be known to you, O king, that we do not serve your gods, nor will we worship the gold image which you have set up."

The Consequence of Obedience

A recently licensed pilot was flying his private plane on a cloudy day. He was not very experienced yet in instrument landing. When the control tower began to bring him in for a landing, he started thinking about all the hills, towers and buildings in that area. Suddenly he began to panic. How would he be able to miss these things if he couldn't see them? In a calm but stern voice the air traffic controller said, "You just obey instructions; we'll take care of the obstructions."

This was the testimony of Daniel's three friends, Shadrach, Meshach and Abed-Nego. They trusted their God to take care of the obstructions. The three obviously would not have chosen to be burned up in a fiery furnace—who would? But they knew that could be the consequence of their absolute obedience to God. The commandments given to Moses centuries before on Mount Sinai clearly forbade the

Jews from worshiping an idol. Their instructions were clear. Their responsibility was obedience; God's responsibility was to take care of the consequences in whatever way He deemed best.

Christians have an equally clear set of instructions. Not only do we have the books of the Old Testament that Daniel's friends would have been familiar with, but we also have the New Testament. Our responsibility is to obey what we know God's Word says and let God deal with the outcome.

Commit your way to the Lord. Be obedient to the clear instructions of God's Word, and let Him deal with any difficulties that might arise. Trust the omnipotent, omniscient God of the universe. Only He can guide you through the obstacles that result from obedience. It's good to know He will.

Obedience is our responsibility; handling the consequences is God's.

Reflections/Prayer Requests

DAY 13

Daniel 3:24–25

*Then King Nebuchadnezzar was astonished;
and he rose in haste and spoke, saying
to his counselors, "Did we not cast three
men bound into the midst of the fire?"
They answered and said to the king,
"True, O king." "Look!" he answered, "I see
four men loose, walking in the midst of the
fire; and they are not hurt, and the form
of the fourth is like the Son of God."*

When Three Become Four

In his book *Healing for Damaged Emotions*, David Seamands wrote, "The day before the [open heart] surgery, a nurse came into my room to visit. She took hold of my hand, and told me to feel it. 'Now,' she said, 'during the surgery tomorrow you will be disconnected from your heart and you will be kept alive only by virtue of certain machines. When the operation is over, you will waken in a special recovery room. But you will be immobile for as long as six hours. You may be unable to move, speak, or to even open your eyes, but you will be conscious. During this time I will be at your side, holding your hand exactly as I am doing now. Although you may feel absolutely helpless, when you feel my hand, you will know that I will not leave you.' It happened exactly as the nurse told me, but I could feel

28

the nurse's hand in mine for hours. And that made the difference!"

As Daniel's friends went through the fiery furnace, they were not alone. When King Nebuchadnezzar looked into the flames, he saw not three but four men walking about. The fourth man in the fire was the Son of God. What these men lost in the adversity of the fiery furnace were the things that had bound them. What they gained was the certain comfort of God's company. The presence of Christ made the difference.

If you are going through a time of fiery testing, let Christ's presence bring you comfort and peace. He will hold your hand. He will walk with you. And when it's over, you will come out stronger and freer than when you went in. Don't fear the fiery furnace; trust God.

Walk with God and you'll never walk alone.

Reflections/Prayer Requests

_____

_____

_____

_____

_____

_____

DAY 14

Daniel 3:27

And the satraps, administrators, governors, and the king's counselors gathered together, and they saw these men on whose bodies the fire had no power; the hair of their head was not singed nor were their garments affected, and the smell of fire was not on them.

God's Protection

No one could say that George Smith didn't have courage. A daring test pilot in the 1950s, back when the sound barrier was first being broken, he could face anything—until he had to bail out of a jet going 805 miles per hour. Though he survived, he was so fearful he thought he might never fly again. Then, during his hospital stay, a nurse gave him an antidote to fear. He took her words to heart when she said, "Courage is knowing the worst—and discovering that, in God's world, the very worst can't really hurt you."

Daniel's three friends experienced the worst that King Nebuchadnezzar could dish out to them. He not only cast them into a fiery furnace but also had the furnace heated seven times hotter than usual. The flames were so deadly that the king's men who cast the three Jewish teens into the fire were themselves consumed by the heat. But when it was all over, God so protected Shadrach, Meshach and Abed-Nego that they emerged from the flames without the smell of smoke on their clothes and without a singed hair on their bodies.

Nothing can happen to a Christian without first passing through the hands of an all-powerful God. Furthermore, He is committed to the protection of those He loves. The psalmist declared, "Therefore we will not fear, though the earth be removed, and though the mountains be carried into the midst of the sea; though its waters roar and be troubled, though the mountains shake with its swelling" (Ps. 46:2–3).

The fiery furnace of affliction can bring you pain and heartache, but it can't cause you eternal harm. God is your protector. You are the apple of His eye (Zech. 2:8), and under His wings you will find safety forever (Ps. 17:8; 57:1). Replace your fears with faith. Enjoy God's protection in your hottest furnace of affliction.

What God protects, nothing harms.

Reflections/Prayer Requests

_____

_____

_____

_____

DAY 15

Daniel 4:26

And inasmuch as they gave the command to leave the stump and roots of the tree, your kingdom shall be assured to you, after you come to know that Heaven rules.

Heaven Rules

One night an admiral on a U.S. Navy battleship ordered a certain course. The navigation officer, seeing a light in the distance, reported that the battleship seemed to be on a collision course with another ship. The admiral immediately ordered his radio officer to send a message to the on-coming ship demanding that it change its course ten degrees to the south. The reply came simply, "No. You change your course ten degrees to the south." After two more unsuccessful exchanges, the admiral, now quite furious, came thundering into the radio control room, grabbed the microphone and bellowed into it, "Change your course. I am a battleship!" After a brief moment of silence, the even-tempered reply came back, "Change your course. I am a lighthouse!"

Nebuchadnezzar was confident that he was the most powerful and important ruler alive. Dozens of lesser kings had challenged his authority, only to be conquered and brought into submission. Therefore, it disturbed him when he was given the vision of a great tree that was chopped down. The prophet Daniel revealed to this mighty despot that great as he was, heaven was greater still. And only after the proud ruler was willing to acknowledge the priority of God would his kingdom be restored to him.

No matter how important and powerful we might be, even as mighty as Nebuchadnezzar himself, we can no more challenge God than a ship can oppose a lighthouse. When God speaks, our best recourse is to submit and obey.

Are you struggling with God? Is there an area of your life that is cause for conflict? Don't crash your life into the rocks beneath the lighthouse. Let heaven rule. Surrender yourself to God and let Him have His way. It will not only preserve your life but will bring meaning to it as well.

To live your life with confidence, let heaven rule.

Reflections/Prayer Requests

_____

_____

_____

_____

_____

_____

DAY 16

Daniel 4:29–31

*At the end of the twelve months he was
walking about the royal palace of Babylon.
The king spoke, saying, "Is not this great
Babylon, that I have built for a royal dwelling
by my mighty power and for the honor
of my majesty?" While the word was still in
the king's mouth, a voice fell from heaven:
"King Nebuchadnezzar, to you it is spoken:
the kingdom has departed from you!"*

Long-suffering Grace

Someone once said, "To become long-suffering, one has to be long-bothered."
This was certainly true of God's relationship with King Nebuchadnezzar.

Even after the king had been warned in
a night vision about his pride, he apparently failed to change his ways. In spite of
knowing what was going to befall him,
Nebuchadnezzar continued to indulge his
arrogant spirit. In his conceit, he refused
to acknowledge that all he had accomplished was by the expressed aid of the
Lord. Yet God, with long-suffering grace,
allowed him 12 more months before
bringing down judgment on him.

God does not sit in heaven and gleefully look for opportunities to bring about
affliction. His desire is for all men to come
to repentance. Peter wrote, "The Lord is
not slack concerning His promise, as

some count slackness, but is longsuffering toward us, not willing that any should perish but that all should come to repentance" (2 Pet. 3:9). Accordingly, He both warns and waits, seeking to bring about change through the conviction of His Spirit rather than the heavy hand of judgment. Only as a last resort does He apply the consequences of sin to those who commit it.

Christians also should be willing to show grace over an extended period of time. Rather than quickly doling out condemnation, we ought to offer ample opportunity for grace. While judgment ultimately must be meted out, give plenty of time for a change of heart.

If you are dealing with a rebel in your life, do so with long-suffering grace. Make sure that you show others the kind of grace that God has demonstrated to you. That's the way to be like God.

Grace shines brightest when it suffers longest.

Reflections/Prayer Requests

DAY 17

Daniel 4:35

All the inhabitants of the earth are reputed as nothing; He does according to His will in the army of heaven and among the inhabitants of the earth. No one can restrain His hand or say to Him, "What have You done?"

An Unrestrained Hand

In 1812 Napoleon proposed to invade Russia and bring its people under his control. When the plans were laid out, someone ventured to say, "Man proposes, but God disposes." On hearing that remark, Napoleon replied, "I propose, and I dispose." His pride, however, proved fatal. Using one of His tiniest, most fragile creations—the snowflake—God brought the proud general to his knees. Bogged down in heavy snow, Napoleon ordered a retreat. His army of 600,000 men was decimated, with fewer than a 100,000 making it back home again. Ultimately, this disaster weakened his armies and brought about his final defeat in 1813.

Napoleon learned what King Nebuchadnezzar also had learned. When God wills it, no one can stop it. After recovering from his seven years of madness, a much humbler king of Babylon declared, "No one can restrain His hand." Even though they led mighty armies and conquered many lands, both of these proud men discovered that God does what He desires and no one says to Him, "What have You done?"

It's a great comfort to those who love the Lord to know that He can be neither intimidated nor defeated. If they are from the Lord, whatever plans we have will unfold no matter who opposes them. Jesus said, "See, I have set before you an open door, and no one can shut it" (Rev. 3:8). Conversely, if your plans are not from the Lord, they ultimately will fail no matter who proposes them.

Prayerfully place your plans and desires into God's hands. Be assured that if they are His will, He will bring them about. Nothing can stop God's will.

No matter what man proposes, it's God who disposes.

Reflections/Prayer Requests

DAY 18

Daniel 5:5–6

*In the same hour the fingers of a man's hand
appeared and wrote opposite the lampstand
on the plaster of the wall of the king's palace;
and the king saw the part of the hand that
wrote. Then the king's countenance changed,
and his thoughts troubled him, so that the
joints of his hips were loosened and his knees
knocked against each other.*

The Fear of God

Man is plagued with many fears, some
of them odd. Mysophobia is fear of dirt.
Hydrophobia is fear of water. Nyctophobia
is fear of darkness. Acrophobia is fear of
high places. Xenophobia is fear of
strangers. Claustrophobia is fear of confined places. Triskaidekaphobia is fear of
the number 13. Unfortunately, many people who have learned to fear things that
they probably shouldn't have never
learned to fear God.

Belshazzar was one of those people.
Whatever other fears he may have had, a
fear of the God of Israel was not one of
them. In the midst of a great feast, the
king, a grandson of Nebuchadnezzar, ordered the gold and silver vessels taken
from the temple in Jerusalem to be put on
display. With utter disregard for the sacred
nature of these utensils, and with no concern for God, Belshazzar profaned them

by using them in his drunken revelry. It was not until a hand appeared and wrote on the palace wall of God's judgment that this arrogant king began to fear. But by then it was too late. His fate was sealed.

Many people today treat God flippantly. They use His name in vain. They trample His standards of righteousness underfoot. They flout their sin in His face. They treat God's people with disdain and contempt. Yet they show no fear. Only when it's too late for many of them will they realize what fools they've been.

Be assured that one day everyone will fear God. The best course of action is to bow before Him in fear as Savior now so you don't have to bow before Him in fear as Judge later. The choice is yours. Choose wisely.

Fear God now and you won't have to fear God later.

Reflections/Prayer Requests

_____

_____

_____

_____

_____

_____

_____

DAY 19

Daniel 5:22–23

"But you his son, Belshazzar, have not humbled your heart, although you knew all this. And you have lifted yourself up against the Lord of heaven. They have brought the vessels of His house before you, and you and your lords, your wives and your concubines, have drunk wine from them. And you have praised the gods of silver and gold, bronze and iron, wood and stone, which do not see or hear or know; and the God who holds your breath in His hand and owns all your ways, you have not glorified."

A Humble Heart

Popular culture has lost its grasp on humility. When asked about the sin of pride, rap singer Queen Latifah replied, "Pride is a sin? I wasn't aware of that." Actress Kirstie Alley added, "I don't think pride is a sin. . . . I think some idiot made that up." And rapper Ice-T responded, "Pride is mandatory. That's one of the problems of the inner city. Kids don't have enough pride." Somewhere along the line these people have neglected reading the Bible. God clearly says that pride is sin.

Belshazzar, the last of Nebuchadnezzar's line to rule Babylon, also fell victim to pride. He surely had heard of his grandfather's experiences, but apparently they made no impression on him. Even though the Medes and the Persians were advancing on his kingdom, he was so confident of his defenses that he spent the evening in revelry rather than preparation. In his arrogance, he gave praise to the gods of materialism and failed to glorify the one true God, who could have saved his life. In thinking that he had it all, he lost everything.

Much of modern society is headed in the same direction. People take great pride in the advancements they've made in medicine, communications and other forms of technology. Yet they've failed to acknowledge that their achievements have been only by the grace of God.

The Bible's advice is still the best. Humble yourself before God. Lift up your accomplishments and confess that they are all gifts from the Lord, who is the giver of all good things (James 1:17). Give thanks to Him who holds your very breath in His hands. Set aside pride and grab hold of God.

All we have we owe to God.

Reflections/Prayer Requests

_____

_____

_____

_____

_____

DAY 20

Daniel 5:24–28

*"Then the fingers of the hand were sent
from Him, and this writing was written.
And this is the inscription that was written:
MENE, MENE, TEKEL, UPHARSIN.
This is the interpretation of each word.
MENE: God has numbered your kingdom,
and finished it; TEKEL: You have been
weighed in the balances, and found wanting;
PERES: Your kingdom has been divided,
and given to the Medes and Persians."*

In God's Scales

Some government officials claim that something has gone seriously wrong with the American judicial system. A few years ago the Heritage Foundation conducted a study that revealed that the average sentence for murder is only 15 years and the murderer is usually out in 1.8 years. A rapist gets an average of 8 years, but he's out in 60 days. Burglars will likely serve only 4.8 days, and within three years 60 percent of them are arrested for another crime. Furthermore, an Arrand Corporation study confirmed that the average inmate has committed 187 crimes before he is ever sentenced.

God's justice, however, suffers no such flaws. His scales are both accurate and just. In the midst of the king's drunken revelry, Belshazzar discovered that God had been very much aware of his sins all along and that the time of restitution had arrived. The fingers of the hand that spelled out his doom left nothing in question. His kingdom had run its course, his soul was found wanting, and the instruments of God's judgment (the Medes and the Persians) were at the door.

Christians can be thankful that even though human justice often fails, God's justice never does. It is complete; no detail is overlooked. Furthermore, it is totally equitable. Those who are wealthy cannot buy their way out of judgment, those who are eloquent cannot talk their way out, and those who are powerful cannot force their way out. In God's courtroom, no one has an unfair advantage.

If you are suffering under an injustice, just hang on. Appeal your case to God. The One who judges both heaven and earth will execute justice for you as well. Trust Him to do what is right in His own time.

God's justice has no loopholes.

Reflections/Prayer Requests

_____

_____

_____

_____

DAY 21

Daniel 6:3–5

Then this Daniel distinguished himself above the governors and satraps, because an excellent spirit was in him; and the king gave thought to setting him over the whole realm. So the governors and satraps sought to find some charge against Daniel concerning the kingdom; but they could find no charge or fault, because he was faithful; nor was there any error or fault found in him. Then these men said, "We shall not find any charge against this Daniel unless we find it against him concerning the law of his God."

An Honest Politician

It's been suggested that to put *honest* and *politician* together creates an oxymoron (two words that contradict each other), and sometimes it does seem that way. A few years ago a cartoon from *The Wall Street Journal* showed a young, freshman congressman saying to an older member, "Hi! I'm a freshman—when do I get corrupted?"

But not all politicians live so fast and loose. Daniel held a high political position. He had been personal advisor to at least three kings (Nebuchadnezzar, Belshazzar and Darius). And certainly he must have had his share of opportunities for financial kickbacks, sexual improprieties and palace intrigues. But even those who hated him confessed that they could "find no charge or fault." He not only professed to walk according to the moral standards of his God, but he practiced them faithfully as well.

Today we stand in great need of men and women who are willing to serve in public office with Christian integrity. Likely someone in politics is subject to greater-than-average temptations. Yet as Daniel demonstrated, God is able to give the moral strength to fulfill such a position honestly and uprightly.

As you exercise your duty in the voting booth, consider the moral character of those you vote for in addition to other qualifications. And search your own heart. Are there skeletons from your past that need to be confessed and removed? Let God make an "honest politician" out of you.

We must never allow honesty and politics to be strange bedfellows.

Reflections/Prayer Requests

DAY 22

*Now when Daniel knew that the writing was
signed, he went home. And in his upper room,
with his windows open toward Jerusalem, he
knelt down on his knees three times that day,
and prayed and gave thanks before his God,
as was his custom since early days.*

Practiced Prayer

During the Revolutionary War, a soldier
who had crawled into the brush was
caught and accused of communicating
with the enemy. His plea was that he had
only gone in there to pray. The gruff com-
manding officer said, "Soldier, are you in
the habit of spending hours in private
prayer?" "Yes, sir," the private replied.
"Then get down on your knees and pray
now!" thundered the officer. Expecting
soon to meet his Savior, the soldier prayed
a simple yet inspired prayer. When he finished, however, the officer said, "You may
go. I believe your story. If you had not been
often at drill, you couldn't have done so
well at review!"

Daniel was facing a similar crisis. His
enemies had convinced King Darius to
sign a decree making it a crime to pray to
anyone but him for a period of 30 days. But
Daniel also was no beginner at prayer.
Long before he found himself in this major
predicament, he had been in the habit of

praying three times a day with his windows open toward Jerusalem. When this decree put his life in danger, it was only natural he would turn to prayer. Prayer got him into trouble, but prayer also would get him out.

For many people, prayer is something to do only during a critical situation. If you're in trouble, you pray; otherwise you leave God alone. But this is foolish. Only the person who has developed an aptitude for prayer during the mundane times of life is able to pray effectively in a crisis. It takes a lot of practice to perform well under pressure, even in prayer.

Don't wait until trouble comes before you pray. Make it a daily habit. Let your voice be so familiar to God that He won't have to ask, "Who's there?"

Prayer is for every day, not just for special occasions.

Reflections/Prayer Requests

_____

_____

_____

_____

_____

_____

DAY 23

Daniel 6:21–23

Then Daniel said to the king, "O king, live forever! My God sent His angel and shut the lions' mouths, so that they have not hurt me, because I was found innocent before Him; and also, O king, I have done no wrong before you." Then the king was exceedingly glad for him, and commanded that they should take Daniel up out of the den. So Daniel was taken up out of the den, and no injury whatever was found on him, because he believed in his God.

In the Eye of the Storm

Hurricanes are whirling storms that can measure several hundred miles in diameter. Their devastating winds begin to be clocked at 74 miles per hour and may exceed 150 miles per hour. Yet in the center of these storms is a space about 20 miles in diameter where everything is perfectly calm. Surrounded by roaring winds and heavy rains, the eye of the storm is a site of serenity and tranquillity.

Daniel occupied such a spot. While confined in a den of lions, he was surrounded by a pride of hungry felines that would have liked nothing better than a good Kosher meal. Yet through the intervention of God's angels, Daniel had nothing to worry about. In the midst of a terrifying situation, he experienced God's perfect peace and calm.

The storms of life are bound to hit all of us at some point. The strong winds of adversity and the heavy rains of affliction show no respect for a person's age or circumstances. Yet in the midst of these trials, God offers to those who have placed their trust in His Son, Jesus Christ, a place of perfect peace and safety. Isaiah testifies, "You will keep him in perfect peace, whose mind is stayed on You, because he trusts in You" (Isa. 26:3).

If you feel like a hurricane is blowing through your life, a hurricane of debt, depression, disease or deprivation, look to God, who is able to keep you in its eye. Cast your cares upon Him, and He will provide a place of rest for your soul.

When you're in a storm, stay close to the eye.

Reflections/Prayer Requests

_____

_____

_____

_____

_____

_____

_____

_____

DAY 24

Daniel 7:1–3

*In the first year of Belshazzar king
of Babylon, Daniel had a dream and visions
of his head while on his bed. Then he wrote
down the dream, telling the main facts.
Daniel spoke, saying, "I saw in my vision
by night, and behold, the four winds
of heaven were stirring up the Great Sea.
And four great beasts came up from the sea,
each different from the other."*

You Can Depend on It

The following statements are taken from official documents, newspapers and magazines widely read during their day. Listen to what the "authorities" had to say:

"Anyone traveling at the speed of thirty miles per hour would surely suffocate" (1840).

"Electric lights are unworthy of serious attention" (1878).

"No possible combination can be united into a practical machine by which men shall fly" (1901).

"This foolish idea of shooting at the moon is basically impossible" (1926).

"To harness the energy locked up in matter is impossible" (1930).

It's obvious that the accuracy of all these "prophecies" left something to be desired. They were all based on human wisdom, and every one of them turned out to be false.

Yet the prophecies Daniel shared were quite different. As he foresaw the rise of these four great beasts, which represent four earthly kingdoms, he was not drawing from his own knowledge and wisdom. Instead, he was relating a vision that was given to him directly from God.

While people may disagree as to which kingdoms these beasts represent, the rock-solid assurance we have is that God is still in control. After describing these frightening apparitions, Daniel proceeded to describe a scene in heaven in which "the court shall be seated, and they shall take away his [the fourth and last beast's] dominion" (v. 26).

If you are frightened by the future, take confidence in this: God is still on His throne and He always will be. The courts of heaven are in session and they will rule in our favor (v. 27). That's something you can bank on.

Fear God and you don't need to fear the future.

Reflections/Prayer Requests

DAY 25

Daniel 7:9–10

I watched till thrones were put in place, and the Ancient of Days was seated; His garment was white as snow, and the hair of His head was like pure wool. His throne was a fiery flame, its wheels a burning fire; a fiery stream issued and came forth from before Him. A thousand thousands ministered to Him; ten thousand times ten thousand stood before Him. The court was seated, and the books were opened.

An Awesome God

Many things in creation are said to be awesome. The Grand Canyon could be described as awesome. The Pacific Ocean can instill a sense of awe. The sweeping mountain ranges of the Alps or the Himalayans or the Rockies inspire awe. But nothing is more awesome than God.

As Daniel turned from a vision of four frightening creatures, representing four powerful earthly empires, he saw a sight that put all these others things in their place. To counterbalance the awesomeness of these man-made kingdoms, he beheld the Ancient of Days, arrayed in garments of white, seated on a throne of fire and surrounded by innumerable worshipers. Suddenly, everything else became insignificant.

It's easy to become overwhelmed by earthly things. They may be awesome in beauty or size. They also may seem awesome in the sense of being threatening. Sometimes our problems are awesome. There are even days when the little tasks of life loom as awesome. At those times we need to step back and get a perspective on what real awesomeness is. We need a fresh view of God.

If you are feeling overawed by earthly things, take time out to worship God. Don't come to Him with your typical inventory of things you want or need. Leave behind your list of prayer requests for others. Instead, come before Him to seek His face alone. Ask Him to reveal Himself to you as He really is—and be prepared to be awed.

God is not just filled with some awe; He is awesome.

Reflections/Prayer Requests

_____

_____

_____

_____

_____

_____

_____

_____

DAY 26

Daniel 9:1–2

*In the first year of Darius the son
of Ahasuerus, of the lineage of the Medes,
who was made king over the realm of the
Chaldeans—in the first year of his reign I,
Daniel, understood by the books the number
of the years specified by the word of the
L<small>ORD</small>, given through Jeremiah the prophet,
that He would accomplish seventy years
in the desolations of Jerusalem.*

The Book of Books

John Wanamaker, an outstanding American businessman of the 19th century, put together one of the most successful careers of his time. When asked what he considered the best investment he ever made, he replied, "I have made large purchases of property in my lifetime involving millions of dollars. But when I was only 11 years old, I made my biggest purchase of all. From my teacher in a little mission Sunday school, I bought a small, red leather Bible. It cost me $2.75. I paid in small installments from my own money that I had earned." John Wanamaker knew the value of the Bible and he lived by it.

Daniel also knew the value of God's Word. While he was studying the "books" (among which was the Book of Jeremiah), he realized God had set a limit on Israel's captivity. While some assumed the Jewish people would never return to their home-land, Daniel discovered in Jeremiah that God had ordained a period of 70 years for the fulfillment of Israel's chastisement. What a joy and encouragement this must have been for the elderly prophet. God had not forsaken His people; Israel would flourish again as a nation.

Much of the Bible has similar solace for God's people. It offers words of comfort (John 14:1–3), joy (1 John 1:4), encouragement (Isa. 41:10) and instruction (Matt. 28:19–20). When we fail to make the Scriptures a daily part of our lives, we miss the greatest resource for living we have been given.

Are you wondering what to do with your life? Are you afraid and uncertain about the future? Are you troubled by guilt and regrets? The Bible has just what you need—answers. Purchasing a Bible is the best investment you'll ever make. Reading it is the best use of your time.

There are many books, but only one can change your life.

Reflections/Prayer Requests

_____

_____

_____

_____

DAY 27

Daniel 9:4-5

And I prayed to the LORD my God, and made confession, and said, "O Lord, great and awesome God, who keeps His covenant and mercy with those who love Him, and with those who keep His commandments, we have sinned and committed iniquity, we have done wickedly and rebelled, even by departing from Your precepts and Your judgments."

Corporate Guilt

American culture places a great deal of emphasis on the individual. Our heritage admires the hardy pioneer who single-handedly carved his farmstead from the wilderness. We have a sense of awe toward the lone gunman of the Wild West who tamed a lawless town. We take as our role model the rugged individualist who made it on his own in the business world. Therefore, we seldom stop to think that God holds us accountable not only for those things we do as individuals, but for the actions of others as well.

Daniel, however, understood very well this concept of corporate guilt. When he went before the Lord in prayer, it was not just a personal and individual matter; it was a group confession. He prayed, *"We* have done wickedly," *"We* have rebelled," *"We* have departed from Your precepts and Your judgments." Daniel personally had been very scrupulous to uphold God's standards. But he accepted his part in the corporate guilt of his people. He confessed national sin as if it were his own.

We may feel that it's unfair of God to hold us responsible for the sins of others. We aren't the ones having abortions, spreading pornography or dealing in drugs. Yet we are part of a group of people that is doing all these things—and much more. As a member of a society, we are responsible for the actions of our society and, in a sense, participate in its sin as well as share in its guilt.

As you pray today, confess your personal sins to God, but do more. See yourself as one who is responsible to confess the sins of your family, your church and your nation. Recognize that you are not only an individual but part of a corporate body.

Sin is everybody's responsibility.

Reflections/Prayer Requests

_____

_____

_____

_____

_____

_____

DAY 28

Daniel 10:12

Then he said to me, "Do not fear, Daniel, for from the first day that you set your heart to understand, and to humble yourself before your God, your words were heard; and I have come because of your words."

Humble Prayer

A young seminary graduate stepped up to the pulpit, very self-confident and immaculately dressed. He began to deliver his first sermon in his first church. There was a problem, however. The words simply would not come out. Finally, he burst into tears and left the platform obviously humbled. Two elderly women were sitting in the front row. One remarked to the other, "If he'd come in like he went out, he would have gone out like he came in."

What's true of preaching is also true of praying. When the messenger from God arrived to speak with Daniel, he assured the prophet that God had responded to his prayers because Daniel had set his heart to understand and to humble himself before his God. Daniel's spirit of humility made him a powerful force with God. As Proverbs reminds us, "Surely He scorns the scornful, but gives grace to the humble" (Prov. 3:34; cf. James 4:6; 1 Pet. 5:5).

A vital key to effective prayer is a humble spirit. Prayer moves the hand of God, but it must be humble prayer. We cannot enter God's presence with a list of demands or a detailed plan that we only want Him to bless. Instead, we must go with open hearts and open hands ready to receive whatever He knows is best for us. We must bow humbly before Him, willing to place ourselves at His disposal to meet His will, whatever that may be. That's the type of attitude that gets God's attention and response.

Consider your attitude in prayer. If you go with a grocery list to be filled or a sense that God somehow owes you an answer, you'll likely come away empty-handed. But if you come to Him recognizing that you do so only by His grace, unworthy to stand before His throne, and yet privileged to come through Christ, then you are ready to pray. Attitude is everything.

Only the humble can get God's ear.

Reflections/Prayer Requests

_____

_____

_____

_____

_____

_____

_____

DAY 29

Daniel 10:13–14

"But the prince of the kingdom of Persia with-stood me twenty-one days; and behold, Michael, one of the chief princes, came to help me, for I had been left alone there with the kings of Persia. Now I have come to make you understand what will happen to your people in the latter days, for the vision refers to many days yet to come."

Powerful Prayer

The English poet and hymn writer William Cowper wrote:

Restraining prayer, we cease to fight:
Prayer keeps the Christian's armor bright;
And Satan trembles when he sees,
The weakest saint upon his knees.

Cowper rightly recognized that Satan fears the prayers of God's people more than anything else.

It's no wonder, therefore, when Daniel began to pray that he encountered spiritual opposition. His prayers actually created a phenomenal battle in the heavens. The angel sent to respond to his prayers was hindered by the "prince of the kingdom of Persia" for 21 days. This "prince" was not a mortal person like Daniel but apparent-ly a fallen angel of great power. It was not until Michael, the angel often associated with Israel, came to help that God's messenger was able to overcome his adversary and deliver his message.

Prayer is often described as simply "talking to God," and that's true. But it's also an act of spiritual warfare. When we pray, we are invading Satan's territory. Through prayer we can defeat the plans of the Devil and bring about events that will glorify God. These are not situations that Satan takes lightly. He will oppose sincere prayer every way he can.

As you bow to pray, recognize that you are undertaking serious business, not just having a little chat with a good friend. You are engaging in hand-to-hand combat with a mortal enemy and crashing through his strongholds to enter the throne room of God. That's an incredible privilege. Don't take it lightly.

Prayer is not a playground; it's a battlefield.

Reflections/Prayer Requests

DAY 30

Willing or Not

In a cemetery in Hanover, Germany, is a grave covered with huge slabs of granite and marble and fastened with heavy steel clasps. It belongs to a woman who did not believe in the resurrection of the dead. Yet she directed in her will that her grave be made so secure that if there were a resurrection, it could not reach her. In time, however, a seed began to grow and push its way out from beneath the slabs. As the trunk enlarged, the stones were gradually shifted and the steel clasps were wrenched from their sockets. But the dynamic life force contained in that little seed is only a faint reflection of the tremendous power of God's creative word that someday will call to life the bodies of all who are in their graves. Willing or not, they will be resurrected.

A messenger from God revealed this same truth to Daniel. As this angelic messenger opened the door to the hallway of time, he revealed to the prophet many things: the rise and fall of various kingdoms, the invasion of the army from the North and, ultimately, the resurrection of the dead. For those who are prepared, whose names are written in the Book of Life, it is a resurrection to everlasting life. For those unprepared, it is a resurrection to everlasting shame and contempt.

This Old Testament message is also echoed throughout the New Testament. The apostle Paul declared that "the dead in Christ will rise first" (1 Thess. 4:16), while the apostle John saw the dead who were "judged, each one according to his works" (Rev. 20:13).

There is no way that you can avoid the resurrection, but you can be ready for it. Make sure that your name is written in the Book of Life. If you haven't done so already, receive Jesus Christ as your Savior and be ready and willing for what is sure to come.

Only a fool fails to prepare for what he knows is coming.

Reflections/Prayer Requests

_____

_____

_____

_____

_____

_____

_____

DAY 31

Daniel 12:3

*Those who are wise shall shine like
the brightness of the firmament, and
those who turn many to righteousness
like the stars forever and ever.*

God's Stars

We are enamored with stars. When Robert Redford was in Santa Fe making a movie, a woman encountered him in an ice cream parlor on Canyon Street. Overcome with awe on the inside, she tried to stay calm on the outside. After leaving the ice cream parlor, however, she realized that she didn't have the ice cream cone she had paid for. Hurriedly she returned to the shop to ask for it. Redford, overhearing the conversation, quietly said, "Madam, you'll probably find it where you put it—in your purse."

God also has stars, but they seldom get the reactions that people like Robert Redford do, at least in this world. Yet God's messenger told Daniel that those "who turn many to righteousness" will shine like the stars for all of eternity. Earthly stars from stage and screen fade away and are forgotten by later generations, but God's stars are eternal.

Righteousness in its simplest form is having a "right relationship" with God. Those who have that right relationship with God through His Son, Jesus Christ, and share with others how they may have such a relationship are God's brightest stars. It's not a matter of being rich or famous. It's not necessary to be on television or in the movies. You don't even have to have a well-known name. All you need to do is share Jesus Christ with others.

Do you want to be a star for God? Do you want to shine forever? Then commit yourself to sharing Christ with others. Find a Gospel tract and become familiar enough with it that you can share it with someone else. Write the story of how you came to know Christ. Ask God to give you the opportunity to share that testimony with others. Let your light shine, and God will make you a star.

Earthly fame is fleeting; God's stars shine forever.

Reflections/Prayer Requests

_____

_____

_____

_____

_____

_____

_____

_____

GIANTS OF THE OLD TESTAMENT

Look for these other titles in the series:

Also coming in 1999: